# Building Community

## Proven strategies
## for turning homeowners into neighbors

THIS PUBLICATION DONATED BY:

GEORGIA CHAPTER
community
ASSOCIATIONS INSTITUTE

FOUNDATION FOR
community
ASSOCIATION RESEARCH

www.cairf.org

Community Associations Press®
Alexandria, VA

ISBN 0-944715-77-X

© 2005 Community Associations Press,® a division of Community Associations Institute.

Community Associations Press
A Division of Community Associations Institute
225 Reinekers Lane, Ste. 300
Alexandria, VA 22314

To order additional copies of this book, please write to the publisher at the address above or call (888) 224-4321. You can also order online at *www.caionline.org/bookstore.cfm*.

*This publication is designed to provide accurate and authoritative information in regard to the subject matter covered. It is sold with the understanding that the publisher is not engaged in rendering legal, accounting, or other professional services. If legal advice or other expert assistance is required, the services of a competent professional should be sought.*—From a Declaration of Principles, jointly adopted by a Committee of the American Bar Association and a Committee of Publishers

Printed in the United States of America

**Library of Congress Cataloging in Publication**

Building community : proven strategies for turning homeowners into neighbors.
    p. cm.
  ISBN 0-944715-77-X
  1.  Homeowners' associations—United States—Management. 2.  Condominium associations—United States—Management. 3.  Housing management—United States.
  HD7287.82.U6B85 2004
  643'.1'0684—dc22
                             2004019861

This book is dedicated to the thousands of volunteers and professionals who care about the well being of their neighbors and clients, who are passionate about improving the quality of life within their associations, and who wish to inspire others to share the responsibility and the rewards of community association living.

# CONTENTS

# ACKNOWLEDGMENTS

AUTHORS

Bill Overton, PCAM

Brent E. Herrington

Robert Schwarting, PCAM

Drew Mulhare, CMCA, AMS, LSM, PCAM

Ronald L. Perl, ESQ.

Lucia Anna Trigiani, ESQ.

Jo-Ann M. Greenstein, CMCA, AMS, PCAM

Bill Greer

P. Michael Nagle, ESQ.

Beth Grimm, ESQ.

PROJECT MANAGER

Andrew Krakowski
Community Associations Institute

EDITOR

Debra H. Lewin, Director
Community Associations Press

DESIGNERS

Mary Prestera Butler, Creative Director
Community Associations Institute

Cori Canady, Art Director
Community Associations Institute

Community Associations Press, the publishing division of Community Associations Institute (CAI), is dedicated solely to publishing the very best resources available for community associations. It publishes the largest collection of books and guides on community associations available today.

Founded in 1973 as a multidisciplinary, nonprofit alliance serving all stakeholder in community associations, CAI is the only national organization dedicated to fostering vibrant, responsive, competent community associations. Our mission is to assist community associations in promoting harmony, community, and responsible leadership.

CAI has more than 16,000 members in 55 chapters throughout the United States. To find out more about CAI, visit www.caionline.org or call CAI Direct at (703) 548-8600 or (888) 224-4321 (Mon–Fri, 9:00–6:30 ET).

# PREFACE

Like a fine wine or an artist's masterpiece, the notion of building community just keeps getting better with age. In fact, as a philosophical movement within the Community Associations Institute (CAI), it has become a full-blown juggernaut and has literally changed the face of the association management industry for the better. This phenomenon can only be explained by accepting the fact that our competitive marketplace, as defined by our customers—the homeowners, demands it.

This has been an interesting process to watch unfold over the last few years. We began with some CAI conference sessions on how to build a sense of community in condominium and homeowner associations rather than focus only on rules enforcement. These sessions were well received by managers, but they clamored for more "how to" information. This feedback set the Institute on the course of developing publications such as *Be Reasonable! How Community Associations Can Enforce Rules Without Antagonizing Residents, Going to Court, or Starting World War III* and *Community First! Emerging Visions Reshaping America's Condominium and Homeowner Associations*. Educational programs such as the M-360 course: "Leadership Practices in Building Community" also were developed. These were big steps that added practical content to CAI's resources for managers. Still, managers asked for even deeper how-to assistance.

CAI went back to the drawing board to meet its customer's needs and came up with the concept for this practical, strategy-oriented guidebook. This book is intentionally designed to be collaborative and anecdotal. Many of the industry's best management and legal practitioners share their successes, their best practices, with you in their own words.

Try out those practices that seem workable for your community and run with them—refine and improve on them. Help us continue to raise the bar as we serve our country in perhaps its most important area—at the grass roots community level.

If September 11th has taught us anything, it's the importance of our connection and interactions as Americans. As such, what higher mission could possibly get us out of bed in the morning than helping people make a difference in their communities? Thankfully, the practical tools to do so just keep on growing at CAI.

Manage well, and with passion for helping people!

*Bill Overton, PCAM*
*Scottsdale, AZ*

# INTRODUCTION

*By Brent E. Harrington*

# Aspiring Beyond Administration
*How to Achieve Social and Civic Well Being*

After working with community associations for nearly 20 years, I have reached the conclusion that all community associations—and the people who lead them—fit pretty neatly into one of two distinct categories: administrative or aspirational. The first (and by far the largest category) comprises what I call administrative associations. They operate under the premise that a community association is essentially a neighborhood housekeeping organization. The association's purpose is to maintain common elements and enforce rules. Thus, the role of management is to furnish competent administration for the maintenance and enforcement operations of the association. The board and the manager in an administrative association tend to regard a high level of resident apathy as a compliment. Residents must be happy if they're not showing up for community meetings or casting votes for board positions. The more invisible and unnoticed the association becomes, the happier its members are presumed to be. Issues of conflict are resolved in a dispassionate, process-oriented manner.

The board's goal, in administrative associations, is to treat every person and every issue in a consistent and uniform fashion. Interaction with such an association tends to feel professional and businesslike. For example, a resident who has an issue to address with the board (his or her neighbors) should not expect to have a neighborly discussion to resolve the matter. Instead, the resident is typically allowed to come before the board and recite his or her case, while the board members remain completely silent and refuse to engage. No conversation about the matter will occur until the resident has physically left the meeting. Only then will the board members discuss the matter among themselves. They will later transmit their verdict to the resident in writing via the U.S. mail. The resident may feel as if they were participating in a tribunal of sorts rather than a meeting of neighbors.

The second and much smaller category is made up of what I call aspirational communities. In this type of association, the role of the board and manager is as much about building the social and civic well-being of the community as it is about maintaining the physical plant or enforcing the rules. Aspirational communities tend to be managed by people who express a sense of passion and idealism about community. These managers and board members believe their role is to provide leadership and inspiration, not merely administration. They strive to engender a sense of caring, civic pride, and shared responsibility. They position the association as a wellspring of resident volunteerism in a wide range of community-related activities, both inside and outside the association's boundaries. Apathy is viewed as a negative characteristic, and community meetings tend to draw very high levels of attendance and participation.

These managers often identify themselves as community managers rather than association managers. In an ironic twist, these managers have learned that their efforts to build a sense of community tend to greatly reduce the number of administrative problems such as rules violations and delinquent assessments. Conflicts in such a community tend to be addressed in a humanistic, compassionate manner. The emphasis is on dealing empathetically with people as neighbors, and appreciating

## FIVE CONCEPTS FOR BUILDING COMMUNITY

■ As a "community builder," you will need perseverance and determination. Not every new initiative or program will be successful. Don't be discouraged when a new project gets off to a slow start. They tend to start slowly and gradually gain momentum.

■ Set a tone that is light-hearted and fun. It should be a joy to be active in the community. Remember to celebrate small victories. Recognition and applause are like rocket fuel for volunteer-based activities.

■ Don't make the community an island. Establish significant points of connection and collaboration with the community at large. Your community can have important, mutually beneficial relationships with area schools, businesses, clubs and leagues, city government, social service agencies, worship groups, activity groups, and more.

■ A significant part of your volunteer activity should be based on helping others in need. Community-based philanthropy or social service projects help engender a deep sense of community pride and embody the highest ideals of community.

■ Build community traditions. In the greatest of communities, residents look forward year after year to major seasonal events and community celebrations. These recurring events create countless memories and become deeply ingrained in the pattern of life in the community.

whatever unique circumstances may exist. The overarching goal is to transform mere housing units into vibrant neighborhoods and communities.

The difference between the two types of associations has little to do with the written word of their CC&Rs; it has everything to do with the values and priorities of the people who lead them. Somehow, those who place a strong emphasis on community seem to transcend the legalistic nature of their governing documents.

In recent years, CAI has worked to elevate community-building as a central component of an association's mission. This book explores the entire concept of building community within the context of the community association. By reading this book, you will learn how residents, board members, and managers can achieve this lofty, but attainable, goal.

On the operations side, Rob Schwarting, a manager of a large community in New York, looks at strategic planning in associations. He provides an inside look at how the planning process, as well as the plan itself, can be used to provide strategic direction and infuse enthusiasm for creating a great community. Bill Greer, of the Southeastern Institute for Research, writes about how surveys can be used to check the pulse of a community and tap into ideas and opinions of residents who may otherwise remain silent. California attorney Beth Grimm looks at alternative dispute resolution and shows how mediation, rather than litigation, solved a tough problem and saved an association $50,000.

From the opposite coast, Maryland attorney Mike Nagle demonstrates how to steer clear of many common problems that plague association meetings. Ford's Colony Vice President Drew Mulhare discusses the roles of the manager, board, and resident in fostering community spirit, and attorney Ron Perl explores community governance systems. To assist in combating one chronic challenge to community associations, Virginia attorney Pia Trigiani provides tips on creating reasonable rules. She shows how this exercise will prevent future conflict and promote community harmony. Jo-Ann Greenstein looks at how volunteer community service projects and neighborhood social gatherings can foster a more vibrant community environment.

## MY PERSPECTIVE

**Brent E. Herrington** is Vice President, DMB Associates, Inc., in Scottsdale, Arizona.

*If you are new to the concept of community building in associations, this book will provide inspiration and know-how to get you started. All the contributors to this book share a common goal: to build stronger, more active, more caring communities.*

*If your experience as a community-builder proves to be anything like my own, I know you'll find the journey to be fun, inspiring, and deeply satisfying. I wish you much success in fulfilling your highest aspirations for your own community.*

# 1

*By Robert Schwarting*

# Strategic Planning
*How One Community Made it Happen*

A few years ago, Radisson Community Association in New York found itself at a crossroads. A series of contentious issues between residents and the developer plus the departure of a long-time manager had rocked the community. An entirely new board of directors was swept into office to deal with the crisis.

The new board—lacking a strategic plan—spent much of its time fighting over insignificant issues and petty power struggles. I feared that our community would lose sight of its mission and that the directors would veer away from policy oversight and toward micro-management. It was time for strategic planning.

Several key community leaders and I challenged ourselves to create a strategic plan for the association that would encompass all parts of the community. We needed a forward looking, positive focus and agreement from everyone. On this foundation we would build the capacity to manage our community effectively.

The entire process—from identifying the leaders to spending the first dollar directed by the strategic plan—took about

12 months. The strategic plan has proven to be—and will continue to be—an extremely useful guide. More important than the document, however, was the effect of the process. By engaging the entire community, we achieved consensus and developed a coordinated movement. A proactive mindset took hold, and we made decisions with confidence.

Residents report that they feel good about the community and believe the leaders are steering Radisson in the right direction. Now that many of the objectives have been achieved, the board has asked the long-range planning committee to fine-tune the plan, set new agendas, reprioritize, and reaffirm the consensus.

Here's how we made it happen.

## Funding the Process

It cost about $5,000 to fund the process, of which about $3,600 covered wages for college students skilled in relational databases, Excel, PowerPoint, word processing, statistical analysis, and presentation graphics. We paid them approximately $6.50 per hour. If staff members are capable of performing these functions, some or all of this expense could be eliminated.

The balance, $1,200, covered survey printing, postage and mailing costs, and meeting expenses. Upgrading our computer software to perform statistical analysis was another $250.

Although postage was relatively high ($780 including return postage), mailing surveys was highly effective. Our initial response was 95 percent. The remaining five percent responded to a follow-up mailing, giving us 100 percent. Surveys printed previously in the newspaper cost less, but responses were spotty and not statistically valid or useful.

Five thousand dollars was a relatively small investment considering the value and long-term benefit derived from this effort.

## Staffing the Process

### Consultants
Some associations hire professional strategic planning facilitators or consultants. This can add another $10,000 to $15,000 to the cost. We were able to avoid this expense because I have experience facilitating strategic planning, as did three members of our

Before deciding to hire an independent strategic planning facilitator, ask yourself these questions.

■ Does the association have sufficient funds for a strategic planning consultant?

■ Does the staff have the capacity for the added workload?

■ Will an internally generated plan have the necessary credibility?

■ Do the staff and key volunteers have experience in small group processes, and are they well versed in the vocabulary and process of strategic planning?

■ Do the staff and volunteers have the motivation to finish the project on time?

long-range planning committee. There are good reasons, however, to consider hiring an outside facilitator.

### Volunteers
We recruited volunteers to enter data in spreadsheets and generate tables that quantified residents' opinions. Some volunteers attended input sessions, wrote reports, and transcribed session notes. They gave about 250 hours over a five-month period.

### Staff
Although students and volunteers did most of the work, the association staff also helped by opening envelopes when the surveys came back and organizing the materials.

### Managers
As manager, I had to clear my desk of other duties for long stretches, and work only on strategic planning—about 200 hours over the course of 12 months. I attended meetings, supervised the college students, and analyzed data to find relationships that I suspected were masked behind other data. For example, the data on our youth programs and facilities revealed no clear answers. But, when we coded by respondent's age, we found the youth had significantly different preferences than the adults.

### Reference Books
Strategic planning is different from the resource driven planning most community managers are familiar with. Driven by the

question "What if?," strategic planning is about transforming the system, not managing it.

We gain knowledge from books. Even though I had experience with strategic planning and facilitating groups in a vision- and goal-setting process, I still found it necessary to review the planning process. Getting started might take more time for managers who don't have experience in the process; but there are plenty of resources available.

## Retooling the Long-Range Planning Committee

The association had a long-range planning committee tasked with addressing both planning and operations. We separated the two functions and asked the operations committee to look at issues we would face in the next 12 months and to plan the facility budgets.

The charter for the long-range planning committee was changed to incorporate strategic planning—examine issues that would affect the community in five to ten years, and monitor issues arising outside the community.

We asked past and current board members to identify and enlist residents for the planning committee—business and non-profit corporation leaders who also had experience in strategic planning. Many of them had already come to my attention, but I knew there were more untapped, talented members in our community. Six people were willing to participate—enough to develop synergy without being unwieldy.

## Empowering the Team

To kick things off, we invited two experts to address our group at a special seminar we called an empowerment session. One was a business administration faculty member at the nearby state college and the other was from the Syracuse City administration. They agreed after we explained the purpose of the long-range planning committee and asked for their guidance. They provided technical knowledge of strategic planning and helped us to think through the process.

More important, the seminar attracted and empowered our core volunteers—mostly board and committee members, but also dedicated residents with planning experience. By the end of

*Simplified Strategic Planning: A No-Nonsense Guide for Busy People Who Want Results Fast!* by Robert W. Bradford and J. Peter Duncan. Chandler House Press, 1999. ISBN 1886284466.

*Strategic Planning for Nonprofit Organizations: A Practical Guide and Workbook*, by Michael Allison and Jude Kaye. John Wiley & Sons, 1997. ISBN 0471178322.

*Creating and Implementing Your Strategic Plan: A Workbook for Public and Non-profit Organizations* by John M. Bryson and Farnum K. Alston. Jossey-Bass, 1995. ISBN 0787901423.

*High Impact Tools and Activities for Strategic Planning: Creative Techniques for Facilitating Your Organization's Planning Process* by Rod Napier, et al. McGraw-Hill Trade, 1997. ISBN 0079137261.

the seminar, three members of the planning committee and six new volunteers had become our strategic planning team.

## Gaining Resident Support

We knew we needed community involvement to achieve success, so we developed a Radisson "Nielsen Panel," named after the group that samples television viewers. By recruiting every ninth resident from our street lists, which included all neighborhoods and housing types, we'd have a statistically reliable sample. They would complete several surveys over the next 12 months.

### Nielsen Panels

We sent each recruit an invitation to participate that described the surveys and specified when they would arrive. Those willing to participate simply returned a postage-paid acceptance card. If a resident declined, we selected the next household. Over the next six months, we sent the sample group two sets of questions.

First we asked them to rate their satisfaction with many aspects of the community like parking, neighborhood cleanliness, and amenities. We also asked them about Radisson's mission and priorities, why they decided to live here, or why they tell friends about the community. Finally, we asked them to rank the relevance of many existing programs and policies.

Several months later, we sent a second set of questions, a list of long-term objectives, program goals, and facility wish lists developed over the previous few months. The purpose was to confirm the work done by residents during the input sessions and by the strategic planning team in organizing and ranking the proposed changes. We wanted the Nielsen Panel to evaluate our progress, rank projects, agree or disagree with statements about the future, and to comment on several objectives. We used their comments to complete the planning process.

### Input Sessions

To gather more information to help develop our vision, we held three input sessions. For the first two, we solicited representatives of different geographic areas, demographics, and committees. About 30 people attended each session; of the 60 attendees, roughly half had been personally invited.

The format for the sessions was a composite of different ideas from the strategic planning books and other examples. We used a modified SWOT approach, focusing on Strengths, Weaknesses, Opportunities, and Threats. We decided not to discuss strategies or lay out a conventional plan; instead, we emphasized inventing change, redefining (or reconfirming) the community mission, and reaching for our dreams.

My role, as facilitator, was to keep the discussion focused on brainstorming and innovation. We began by reviewing the ground rules: be positive and encourage everyone to contribute. We followed with an "icebreaker," in which participants described their ideal community. We brainstormed as a full group, and we brainstormed in smaller groups.

Using flip charts, we sorted and organized all ideas under the headings of visions, goals, objectives, threats and opportunities, strengths and weaknesses, major strategic groupings, the strategic plan, guidance to committees, and establishing a repetitive annual goal-setting and budget-planning process.

About 60 ideas emerged from the two sessions. They included recruiting and electing residents to local boards and agencies; re-evaluating the architectural guidelines to provide more flexibility, involving community youth in governance, creating a wellness center; and promoting increased interaction and connectivity among residents.

The strategic planning team met to analyze and organize these ideas. At a follow-up session with the original group, the team proposed five major areas of strategic focus:

- The "new community" philosophy
- Health and wellness
- Secure, friendly, and attractive community
- Arts and culture
- Enforcing, maintaining, and amending the covenants

We convened a third input session to develop strategies for these five areas, and participants prepared a report for the board that contained many comments about our youth. Consequently, the board added a sixth area of strategic focus on youth. The board also reaffirmed the consensus-building effort and encouraged the team to solicit more input from the community.

**Community Poll**

We asked roughly 250 residents—again representing all ages, social groups, and locations—how they felt about our proposed programs, facilities, and actions. The responses confirmed our plans and helped us prioritize our actions. Youth and teen-related programs were given the highest priority, as were two proposed facilities—a YMCA-like center and an adult clubhouse with restaurant. We asked for additional comments from the community using the community newspaper, but we received very little feedback. Backed by all the data, the board and committee leaders now had confidence in the strategic plan. The board formally accepted it, and we began integrating it into the budget process.

## A Strategic Plan and Much More

After all our work, we'd developed a concise planning document with articulated visions and goals to guide our community into a successful future! It provided direction and outlined projects and paths that were preferred by the community. While this alone was a tremendous accomplishment, there were other, more significant, outcomes:

- We got a better picture of the community and formed relationships with other people and neighborhoods.
- Three new directors emerged, and two long-time residents became active on behalf of the community.

- Leaders and residents became positive and confident.
- Absolutely no one objected to the budget and assessment increases.
- The board focused its energies on strategic issues, not on nitpicking the standards or on disputing the developer.

The board and committees had a path to pursue, and they began moving forward as the plan was being written. The survey results gave them confidence in their plans to change the budget and make commitments to raise capital for new programs without any second-guessing.

Overall, the board, committees, and residents acted more professionally and felt they were in control of their destiny.

## The Future

This was the right process for our community at the time. During the next round of planning, however, we will cast the net wider, searching for participants from outside of the community. We are looking for some truly strategic thinking about very difficult local and regional issues, such as town zoning and school site policy, in which the community association has a serious vested interest.

In this cycle, there will be more small-group meetings. The costs could be twice as much because we will need to hire experts to assist. Also, we will create small action groups that will fully develop ideas and plans for large-scale projects before they are brought to the community for adoption. This will involve a major commitment of time. We're considering riding stables, a health and wellness facility, a clubhouse by the river, and a boat park, all of which will require about $10 million, roughly four times the capital assets of the association, or nine times the annual budget.

Using strategic partners from outside the community will greatly reduce the risk for the association. For example, if we involve planners as well as local school and government leaders in creating the future for Radisson, they will likely think more like a member of the community. As stakeholders at the planning table, they will feel more responsible for making Radisson's visions come true. It's critical, therefore, that the planning process includes all potential outside partners. It will also be important that the group remains focused on developing concrete, workable action plans.

Overall, I expect the next cycle of planning to be more rigorous than the first, which was a good preparatory exercise. It was a positive experience for most of the participants and the community as a whole. It accomplished many of the easy tasks and got people dreaming about expensive or threatening changes.

We are proud that a solid foundation for strategic planning has been put into place. Outside stakeholders (the town board, the school board, the county planning agency, and several other local non-profit agencies) saw Radisson's success with strategic planning, and they're looking forward to being involved.

Each year we remind the community about the strategic plan. We've told them the initial objectives have been achieved, and a new cycle of community input and planning is about to start.

## MY PERSPECTIVE

**Robert Schwarting** was Manager of Radisson Community Association in Baldwinsville, New York, a planned community with more than 2,000 homes, when this chapter was written.

*Strategic planning allows community associations to assess their current reality, identify existing challenges, and brainstorm, discuss, dream, and ultimately create a forward-looking vision of a community's future. Strategic planning—both the process and the plan—opens dialogue among the board, staff, residents, and other stakeholders that results in a stronger, more unified community.*

*In my experience, the strategic planning process is the best way to get people involved and to develop programs that have a high probability of succeeding. This type of grassroots organizing and public involvement process is extremely important in giving people a voice and in building community.*

*By Bill Greer*

# Market Research Techniques for Community Associations
*How to Gather the Data You Need to Make Decisions*

Association boards often wonder how unit owners and residents will vote on an issue, or how strongly members feel about specific matters that board members will be voting on at upcoming meetings. Professional market research techniques can be helpful in gauging how residents feel about an issue. It's also an integral tool for strategic planning.

## Quantitative vs. Qualitative

Quantitative market research is used to accurately project data to an entire group (such as a community association) based on sampling the opinions of just a few. Sample respondents can be chosen entirely at random from the larger group (or universe, as it's called in market research), to lessen the labor intensity and cost, while still providing reliable data. This is the generally accepted research method that is used widely today by pollsters and opinion research companies.

On the other end of the market research spectrum is a census—an attempt to gather data from every household. For example, an association of 900 households would attempt to gather data from every one of the 900 households. This is typically a more costly method. Yet, using the more practical random sampling method, if only 200 of those 900 households were polled, the data would have a maximum error factor of approximately seven percent. Therefore, without spending the time and money to survey everyone in the community, a board could *project* the data gathered from the smaller sample (of 200) to the community at large with a strong degree of reliability.

Qualitative market research involves gathering anecdotal information from a smaller group, often very much in depth. Focus groups are a well-known example of the qualitative method. They provide an excellent means of exploring issues from every angle, with lots of valuable information coming from a handful of participants. As an example, imagine a beachfront community association in which some houses are on the ocean side and some on the sound side. The board has the opportunity to add a clubhouse between the two. It would be worthwhile, in this case, to convene a couple of focus groups from each side to determine how similar or different their needs and wants might be—prior to making an investment.

## Data Gathering Techniques

Professional research organizations gather quantitative consumer data in a variety of ways—by telephone interviews, through mail-back surveys, intercept interviews at malls or events, and now even with Internet-based surveys.

Few associations will have the budget to hire an outside firm; therefore, some decisions must be made about how best to gather data. Telephone surveying is labor intensive, and many associations may not be able to enlist enough reliable volunteers for telephone interviewing duty. Internet-based surveys tend to get high response rates, but the technical talent needed to properly program a survey into a format that would be interesting and navigable is expensive. And, although the numbers are growing, not all households are wired.

**Low Cost Surveys**
Surveys can be printed and made available at the association office or at some central location for residents to pick up. A note of caution here: someone could pick up multiple copies of a questionnaire and fill them all out anonymously. This would, of course, seriously bias the results of an otherwise good survey.

Associations can also publish a simple questionnaire in their newsletter. This has several advantages: first, every voting member presumably gets the opportunity to have their say in this census-type survey. Second, the newsletter is going out anyway, so no extra expense is incurred for delivery. Members can be instructed to drop off the completed questionnaire at a convenient central location, avoiding the cost of return postage.

An accompanying newsletter article (or letter from the president) would encourage participation by explaining the board's need for owner feedback. The letter should underscore the anonymity of the response. Whereas many associations have raise-your-hand votes that are seen by all, a mail-in survey is anonymous and encourages members to be candid. It's also important to establish a deadline when all responses must be returned.

A survey such as this can also be used to build attendance at an annual meeting, for example, in which the findings will be disclosed and discussed.

**Professional Moderators for Focus Groups**
As for qualitative data gathering, as in focus group research, a professional moderator may be the key to success. Moderators are available as consultants in most large cities (look under "research" or "market research" in the Yellow Pages). A board member, however, may have had some job experience as a facilitator that would transfer well to this function because the moderator's role is really one of facilitation. He or she will first draft a moderator's outline, covering the issues the board would like to discuss in 90-minute sessions. The board should review and comment on the moderator's outline prior to the session.

Most research firms will set up a video camera to record each session (participants must be notified they are being recorded.) Board members then can watch the proceedings in an adjacent room via video monitor to study the conduct of the group without interfering with the moderator's handling of the session. Confidentiality (beyond the board viewing of results) must be ensured in order for participants to feel they can be candid. Research firms will also provide a written report to the association drafted by the moderator.

## Bias

Professional market research is, at best, an artful science since bias comes from many directions. Even national news can bias survey responses quite dramatically, as was the case just after the September 11th tragedies. However, most potential bias can be dealt with in the design of the research.

It is said that responses are not biased, but all too often, the questions are. Survey instructions should be clear and understandable. Questions should not be confusing, or worse, leading. Good questionnaires have a natural rhythm, often starting with a good introduction, moving from easy questions to more difficult ones.

The same holds true for focus groups. The moderator starts slow and easy, introduces everyone, concisely introduces the subject matter, and later moves into the bigger issues, when the participants are warmed up, receptive to discussion, and engaged.

Most professional research firms will carefully pre-test questionnaires with a short sample to see if they cause any confusion. Internet-based surveys are sometimes tested by friends and family just to see how smoothly they run.

## Some Sample Questions

Most respondents will be candid in surveys, but it's always a good idea to structure questionnaires in a way that prevents misinterpretation. Closed-ended questions (simple yes or no questions) are straightforward and limit misinterpretation.
*Do you believe that security is a community issue at this time? Yes. No.*

Multiple-choice questions are also closed-ended, but sometimes include an open-ended option:

*Which two of the following security measures do you believe to be most effective?*
*a. warning signs at community entrance*
*b. security patrols at night*
*c. security patrols during the day*
*d. adult education about personal security measures*
*e. children's education on security*
*f. other: _____*

Questions that involve a rating can be valuable in measuring strength of belief:

*On a scale of 1–5, where 1 = not at all important, and 5 = very important, how important is it for your community association to be addressing security at this time? 1 2 3 4 5*

Sometimes, a follow-up open-ended question can better define the issues at hand:

*If you circled "4" or "5" in the question above, why is it that you say that security is now "somewhat" or "very" important?*

Even without tabulating the open-ended questions, and simply generating a list of the verbatim responses, the board can get a sense of what concerns are foremost in the minds of residents.

## Tabulation

Professional research firms tabulate data relatively quickly and easily using rather expensive computer software that is designed specifically for this purpose. This allows the board to analyze the data soon after the interview. Large associations will likely need this sophisticated tabulation and should consider hiring a research firm to conduct surveys.

Smaller associations will need to tabulate their data by hand, question-by-question, response-by-response. This requires diligence and attention to detail. It may be that the association can mobilize a group of volunteers from the community to make the work go more quickly.

If you gather certain demographic information (such as how long someone has lived in the community, education level, number of children in the family, household income), the cross-tabulation of this data with the base questions can be of tremendous value in presenting the results. Using the previous example, cross tabulation may reveal that the most security conscious residents tend to be those with children, residing primarily in only two of five neighborhoods. With this kind of data on hand, the board can make better decisions on how to deal with the issue.

## Using the Data

Compelling data that is carefully gathered and well presented can be a powerful tool in managing any association. Often, a survey gives residents an opportunity to write a report card that rates how the board is doing, issue by issue. This is an excellent way for the board to learn where it needs to concentrate its efforts. In fact, most marketing research conducted for corporate clients provides the basis for informed marketing and strategic planning decisions.

Some associations will conduct the same survey every couple of years, so that data can be tracked and performance over the years can be compared. For tracking studies such as this to be fair, the questions must be asked in exactly the same way as in the past. Other questions—on current issues—can be added to the subsequent surveys so that they provide new information as well.

## Using a Consultant

Professional research firms will be generous with their time, especially for nonprofit organizations such as community associations that show an interest in conducting research correctly. It might be a good idea to have two or three representatives of the association call on several research firms to discuss a project and listen to the firm's presentation about what methods they would recommend. This is a valuable learning process, even if the association ultimately decides to go it alone.

Most research firms also will be willing to perform less-than-full-service professional work for your association, for a less-than-full-service fee. For example, the association could negotiate a fee to have such a firm design the questionnaire, then tabulate, analyze, and report on the findings that you gather from your members or residents. This eliminates what often is the most labor-intensive and costly step in the process—the data collection.

# THE COST OF PROFESSIONAL RESEARCH FIRMS

These two fictional examples provide a rough estimate of the expense involved in using a professional research firm.

**Scenario 1.** Sleepy Hollow Homeowner's Association wanted to develop a strategic plan to guide their budget and provide direction for the next five years. The association had 5,000 units, and they decided to do a random mail sampling. They hired a professional research firm to handle all aspects of the project—designing and mailing the survey, tabulating the results, and presenting their analysis and recommendations at an association meeting.

*Cost estimate: $12,000 to $15,000. Note: the cost would be about the same if the survey was conducted by phone, using trained interviewers.*

**Scenario 2.** Landmark Towers Condominium Association (500 units) had requests from unit owners to install a basketball court so that youth in the community would have a safe place to play. Another group of unit owners wanted the association to install a tot lot. They only had enough resources for one project and wanted to survey the residents to see which one should be funded this year. They chose to conduct a census and hired a research firm to develop the questionnaire and tabulate "top-line" results only. The association used volunteers to distribute the survey, and they didn't require much analysis of the results because the questions were primarily closed-ended ones.

*Cost estimate: $2,000 to $2,500.*

## MY PERSPECTIVE

**Bill Greer** was Director of Client Services with Southeastern Institute of Research (SIR) in Richmond, Virginia at the time this chapter was written.

*Solid research need not be arduous or expensive. If conducted and reported properly, the members will applaud the board for using this tool and will see that the data can provide solid guidance for the future.*

CHAPTER

# 3

*By P. Michael Nagle,*
*ESQ.*

# Good Meetings Make Good Neighbors
*How to Increase Morale and Encourage Attendance*

The way an association conducts it meetings and how and when it provides notice of those meetings has a significant effect on the success of a community association. Most association bylaws contain the details of how to do it correctly, and complying with them will go a long way to promote harmony in a community. Let's look at some examples.

The owners at Diamond Farms Condominium were up in arms and determined to oust a board they believed wasn't doing its job. Clearly, there was little harmony in this association. The owners circulated a petition, obtained more than the minimum number of signatures, and sent the petition to the board president. Adhering to the bylaws, the president called a special meeting precisely for the purpose stated in the petition: "to discuss the removal of the board of directors." Following a heated discussion, someone called for a vote to remove the board. But, the petition and the meeting notice only stated that removing the board would be discussed, not voted on.

Diamond Farms' bylaws require that no business be conducted at a special meeting that wasn't specified in the notice, and they require that directors be notified of any meeting called to vote on their removal. Neither of these requirements was met; and, as a result, the owners were not entitled to vote to remove the board at the meeting that night.

A board can't take action that isn't specifically stated in the notice because owners will attend based on what's taking place. If the board conducts business that no one knew about before the meeting, it disenfranchises those who didn't attend. In effect, they didn't receive notice.

Special meeting notices must be written very carefully. Imprecise language can render the meeting invalid. More important, a community already in turmoil could have been further divided by an invalid vote.

## Giving Notice

This example emphasizes the importance of proper notice for special meetings, but notice is equally important for all meetings. Association bylaws and, frequently, state law specify how, when, and to whom notice must be given. Let's look at another example.

### Website Notices Don't Click

The Seventh Circle Homeowners Association president, a computer geek, was very proud of the new association website he'd created. He announced it in the newsletter. Later, when it was time to send out notice of the association's annual meeting, he put it on the website rather than mailing it. The 150-home community needed a quorum of only ten percent, which was barely met when 17 people showed up. Being the annual meeting, attendees elected three of the five board members. When the election results were published in the next newsletter, more than 60 owners claimed they weren't notified of the annual meeting, and they threatened to sue if the election wasn't conducted again. By failing to comply with the meeting notice requirements in its documents, the board had also failed to build community.

Where did Seventh Circle go wrong? It was the means of delivery of the notice that was the problem. According to state law and association documents, delivery by first-class mail, postage prepaid, is almost always permissible—indeed, preferable to registered or certified mail, which many people decline.

There are other ways to deliver meeting notices, but each has its pros and cons. Website postings are free, but not everyone sees them. Hand delivery saves postage, but postal regulations don't allow anything but official mail in a mailbox. Doorstep delivery is economical, but notices may get blown away or rain soaked. Posting notices on bulletin boards, doors, and elevators is common, but people overlook them or may be away when they're posted. Another option is publishing the notice in the association newsletter. This is acceptable only if the notice is prominently featured and the newsletter is sent first-class mail.

These alternative delivery means can be very effective as reminders, but they should be used to call attention to the notices already sent by first-class mail. As reminders they will increase attendance at the meeting, which will promote a sense of community among members.

### Who Needs to Know?

Virtually all bylaws and state laws require associations to notify each owner (including co-owners), even those ineligible to vote at the meeting. This is an effective incentive for owners to clear a delinquency if they want to vote or stand for election.

It's the association's duty to keep an accurate mailing list of owners, and it's the owner's duty to let the association know who and where they are. The association isn't at fault if an owner doesn't receive a meeting notice because he or she failed to notify the association of an address change.

In some cases, meeting notices must be sent to mortgagees as well, particularly when they're affected by a vote at the meeting —like amending the governing documents.

### A Date to Remember

How far in advance of a meeting a notice is delivered is just as important as how it's delivered. Again, state laws and association bylaws will specify the time frame. Usually they only require a minimum time for notice of both annual and special meetings, but some specify a maximum for notice of special meetings. Too much advance notice can be a problem—owners may forget the date or lose the notice if it's delivered too far ahead. As a result, the association may fail to achieve a quorum.

## The Importance of a Quorum

A quorum is the minimum number of owners who must be present at an owners' meeting, in person or by proxy, before business can be transacted. State law or the association's documents will specify the number, and it will vary from one association to another.

The quorum should be as low as possible to conduct business. Low quorum requirements don't discourage attendance, and they give the association the opportunity to have a meeting and conduct business—even if a large percentage of owners do not attend.

### When There's No Quorum

The association must make a reasonable effort to conduct a valid annual meeting. Deciding what's reasonable will depend somewhat on the association's governing documents and how much effort the association made to hold the meeting. Given the importance of the business normally conducted at annual and other meetings, the association should make a concerted attempt to obtain a quorum before abandoning a meeting.

When there's no quorum, a majority of the owners present must vote to adjourn and reconvene at a later date. Since even fewer residents are likely to attend the reconvened meeting, the chair should ask everyone to execute a proxy before leaving.

## Parliamentary Procedure

Some association documents require associations to use parliamentary procedure at annual and special meetings. Many associations follow *Roberts Rules of Order*, which is available in a variety of forms and editions. Because associations rarely need the complicated rules that are contained in complete editions of *Roberts Rules of Order*, abbreviated editions that focus on the basics can be easier to use.

Whether the association uses Robert's or some other rules of order the objective is to conduct civil, productive, and legal meetings. Without them business doesn't get conducted, and the community begins to suffer.

## Board Meetings

More association business occurs at board meetings than at owner meetings because most of the powers and duties of the association are delegated to the board—maintaining property, hiring and firing personnel and contractors, keeping the books and records, developing and enforcing rules, budgeting and setting the annual assessment, formulating policies, and complying with local, state, and federal laws, ordinances, and regulations. Effective, well-run board meetings will contribute significantly to an association's efforts to build community.

### Notice to Board Members

Board members have the same right to proper notice as owners. Older documents require that notice be delivered via U.S. mail three to five days before the meeting. Others allow the board to determine how and when notice should be given. Many boards set the date for the next meeting before adjourning the current one, thereby giving notice at that time. Others set regular monthly meetings for the same day, time, and place (third Tuesday, 7:00 p.m., in the clubhouse) so that it's only necessary to give notice once a year.

Whatever method is used (e-mail, facsimile, telephone, or others), it should comply with the association documents or state law and be given to each director in a timely manner. If no method or time is set by the documents or statute, the board should set its own policy so that there is no dispute concerning whether proper notice was given.

### A Board Quorum

A board quorum differs from a quorum of owners. A board quorum comprises a majority of all directors. Without a quorum, the board can't conduct business or make binding decisions.

Once a quorum is achieved and a meeting is in session, actions can be authorized by a majority of the directors present. Thus, if three of five board members (a quorum) are at a meeting, two of them (a majority) can make decisions for the association.

The proviso in *Robert's Rules of Order* that the president should only vote to break a tie doesn't apply to community associations. If the president is an elected director, he or she must vote on all matters before the board as part of his or her fiduciary obligation to the association. Appointment to the presidency doesn't supersede the obligation to the owners.

### No Proxy Voting for Boards

Each member of the Columbia Association board of directors, also known as the Columbia Council, is elected by the residents of one of the ten villages in Columbia to serve as their representative. Board members routinely give each other their "proxy" when they cannot attend a council meeting. This practice has existed for years, but the charter of the Columbia Association doesn't specifically authorize it.

Unless there is a very specific authorization in the documents or in state laws, board members may not vote by proxy. Each director is elected to vote on behalf of all constituents. The director is, therefore, already voting for that constituency as their proxy. That proxy cannot be further assigned without the consent of every constituent.

By continuing this practice, the Columbia Association may face a problem if a crucial vote is ever challenged.

### Conducting Board Meetings

Some meeting rules say the president or chair sets the agenda. Obviously, the person setting the agenda controls the meeting, although one of the first items on any agenda should be approving the agenda, which allows others to contribute discussion items. It's not unusual for the manager to set the agenda, since he or she is most familiar with the association's current business.

An agenda ensures that all business is conducted, and it keeps the meeting on track. Some boards allot a certain amount of time to each agenda item—ensuring that the entire meeting is concluded within, for example, two hours. Board members will become less focused after two hours.

### Ballots

Few documents or laws specifically require boards to vote by written ballot. Most boards vote verbally or with a raised hand

Most states have "sunshine laws" that require boards to conduct open meetings that can be observed by all members of the association. Only under certain circumstances, can boards conduct closed meetings or convene an executive session.

A board meeting isn't open to owners unless they know about it, but few laws or documents specify how and when to notify them. Associations can simply give owners the same notice as directors; however, if that's too time consuming or costly, the association can issue one annual notice of pre-set monthly board meetings.

because it's practical, fast, and easy to record in the meeting minutes. Sometime a secret, written ballot is appropriate—the election or removal of officers, for example—to avoid acrimony. The board should establish procedures and rules regarding the process and when it will be used.

### The Owners' Voice

Although sunshine laws require associations to notify owners of board meetings, this doesn't give owners the right to participate in the meeting. Many boards find it politic to provide a time for owners to make comments during an "owner forum" at the beginning of the meeting. This has two advantages. First, the board can add to the agenda issues raised by homeowners; and, second, owners are more likely to sit quietly during the rest of the meeting once they've been heard.

Set limits on the time each resident may address the board. After everyone has spoken, make it clear that the remainder of the meeting is the business meeting of the board and that owners are not allowed to speak again.

### The Board Chair

The board president usually conducts board meetings, but he or she can delegate this to another person. Whoever conducts, or chairs, a meeting must be organized, composed, even-tempered, equitable, and in charge without being overbearing. He or she should not be confrontational, dictatorial, inflexible, or egotistic.

The chair is a meeting facilitator and should take advantage of advisors like the association manager or attorney, or experts like architects, engineers, and accountants. The success of the meeting may depend on the presence of the right advisors or experts.

Board meetings need not, and should not, be a one-person show. The board chair should make good use of committee chairs, officers, and directors who can answer questions or explain issues or actions. At the same time, the chair cannot allow others to take over the meeting.

The chair is also responsible for monitoring the discussion and keeping directors on the topic and within the time allotted on the agenda. When discussion becomes tentative, repetitive, or meandering, the chair should ask "Are we ready to vote on the question?" rather than, "Is there any more discussion?" which may foster more fruitless dialog.

The democratic process is alive and well in community associations! However, the process does require order, as well as rules for procedure and behavior so that boards and the owners can work together to preserve, protect, and enhance the value of their property and maintain a strong sense of community.

## MY PERSPECTIVE

**P. Michael Nagle** is an attorney with Nagle & Zaller, P.C., in Columbia, Maryland.

*Association meetings should foster a spirit of community, and association leaders should always try to create a friendly, neighborhood atmosphere at each meeting. Doing so has the dual benefit of increasing community morale and encouraging people to attend future meetings so that obtaining a quorum is not so difficult.*

*A well-organized meeting will be palatable to attendees; when the meeting flows smoothly, people don't feel that their time was wasted by a lot of confusion or unnecessary gyrations. At the same time, it's important that the meeting be flexible enough to accommodate the true needs of the community. For example, some documents have a pre-set agenda for the annual meeting that schedules the election last. Because people usually want to know the results before they leave, I recommend that the chair entertain a motion to move the election to the top of the agenda. This way, the ballots and proxies can be counted while the other business is conducted and, likely as not, the results announced before the end of the meeting.*

*Finally, it's crucial that every procedural requirement of state law and your governing documents be followed to the letter. Your lawyer or association manager is not just being difficult. A challenge based on procedure can land the association in court; and a courtroom is the last place a board or an association can promote harmony or build a sense of community.*

CHAPTER

4

*By Jo-Ann M. Greenstein,*
CMCA, AMS, PCAM

# Community Spirit
*How to Create It in Your Association*

I have been working for well over a decade for an association
that was built during the mid-1980s. This community was
founded by active, young seniors and was once one of the
most desirable adult communities on the Jersey shore. It had a
reputation as a place where neighbors were friendly, amenities
were plentiful, and activities were well attended. In short, the
community had a lot of spirit.

Much to my dismay, I noticed a few years ago that many of
our traditionally popular activities—our annual evening dinner
dance and recreational programs—weren't drawing the high
attendance of years past. This seemed to affect the overall
morale of the community. I also noticed that the common
areas were not buzzing with activity as they used to be, and
the residents didn't seem to be as bubbly. What could it be?

As I contemplated that question in my office one night, my
eyes wandered to a picture on the wall depicting a scene of

happier days in this association. The photograph was taken at the pool with all of the residents surrounding me while I held my two-year-old son. That's when it hit me—my son is now 19! I looked closer and saw all of the fresh, young faces of the residents. Gosh they looked good back then! But wait—I don't look that different. There's no way that I have aged as much as everyone else. Have I? Once I got over the shock that I've celebrated many birthdays since then, the realization set in that the residents have aged, but the social activities haven't adapted to their changing needs. That's why community spirit has suffered, and that's when we set out to reassess our programs.

## Recognizing the Problem

The association has an established board, committees, social infrastructure, and professional management. The social activities committee is guided by and proudly implements its mission statement: "To provide diverse activity and foster community spirit and assistance to members of the association and to serve the needs of our greater surrounding community."

The social activities committee has four sub-committees: the functions committee plans and organizes social gatherings; the game committee organizes indoor and outdoor sporting events and card games; the sunshine committee organizes fund drives and donation campaigns to benefit local charities, and the operations committee monitors and implements maintenance requirements for the social activities, infrastructure, and buildings.

Sometimes a challenge like aging and apathy escapes attention when the day-to-day operations seem to be working fine. Very often, managers and committee members focus on the obvious and not the underlying root causes of problems, which tend to be subtle and expand slowly over time.

In this case, the community had become apathetic. Social functions that were geared toward promoting community spirit and a sense of neighborhood had low participation—and the root cause was a failure to revisit the association's strategic plan on a regular basis.

The plan, which included this goal statement: "To develop a financially secure community association which services the needs of its members operationally and socially," along with the mission statement of the social activities committee needed to be updated. The goals were still applicable, yet the direction needed to be shifted so that the association could meet the evolving needs of the community. The epiphany was that not only were the bricks and mortar of the community association aging, but so too were its residents!

As with any idea, certain experiments need to be run and data gathered before changes are recommended. This was especially the case with us because the residents tended to be conservative and reluctant to change their pattern of living. Discussing the proposed changes would also highlight the fact that the average resident age in the community was increasing. Turnover was not having an impact on the age demographics, but the types of activities that were once popular were being replaced by more sedate activities. The residents' idea of a good time had changed. New needs were emerging regarding quality of life and helping residents to remain comfortable.

The real issue came to our attention when the township sponsored a senior outreach program. The outreach program focused on a variety of health-enhancement and assistance programs available to our community as free services. The social activities committee had promoted the outreach program in the same manner as other programs. However, instead of seeing the same trend of declining attendance, the committee saw that this program generated a standing-room only attendance. The members requested more daytime programs of this nature.

A follow-up program, presented by a local bank, addressing savings, lending, refinancing and a hands on demonstration of state-of-the-art banking (i.e. debit cards, ATM cards, and on-line banking) was also a complete success.

It was now clear to the social activities committee that including new programs that were more educational and less physical was indeed in keeping with the community's mission statement.

A strategy meeting of the board and manager was called to set forth a "New Direction for the New Millennium." The board asked the committees for their assistance in revamping the community programs and agendas. The operations sub-committee was directed to inspect and recommend replacements for old, outdated furniture, taking advantage of lightweight plastics for tables and chairs for better portability and mobility. The sub-committee also was charged with upgrading old pool railings with new assisted lifts, and with replacing the exercise equipment with cardiovascular and low-impact aerobic devices.

The functions sub-committee was given the task of working with the township's senior outreach center to bring in additional speakers and programs on the services available to residents. The group continued to provide fun evenings to the community, such as dinners and dances, but group members were now mindful of the fact that many of the members had become widows and widowers, who may not attend such functions if they were costly or perceived to be for couples.

The sunshine sub-committee took on the task of "doing for *ourselves* as well as others outside our immediate HOA community." The sub-committee established a telephone chain named "Making New Friends" to contact new homeowners and people living alone, upgraded emergency contact lists, and compiled medication and health information about each resident that they placed in the same location in each home to enable emergency medical providers to find it immediately.

The games sub-committee combined men's and women's events where participation was low and added a computer-learning center by recruiting grandchildren (now in their late teens and twenties) to teach members how to use e-mail and the Internet. Grandchildren were paid $25.00 a day.

## Activity Planning

We create a file for each social event in which we keep relevant information such as:
1. Date and time of the event.
2. Name of the chairperson or those who were active in organizing and running the event.
3. Description of how the event was publicized. (For example, in which newspapers did we place classified ads for the community garage sale or which cable access channels announced the event at no charge?)
4. An itemized expense account and receipts for expenditures. (For example, food, beverage, decorations, favors, door prizes, or gifts.)
5. An itemized account of ticket sales or attendance fees. This

list included names, addresses, telephone numbers, and e-mail addresses of attendees. After fundraising events, this list is important so that thank you letters can be mailed.

6. Suggestions from those who attended. (For example, could it be better next time, should it become an annual event, or was the event what was expected?)

These files are reviewed carefully during an activities planning session in which the social activities committee, board, and community manager compile an activity calendar for the following year. The annual calendar is published and provided to the community. We list the events in a computer calendar program, and on the 20th of each month, the following month's calendar of events is distributed as a reminder. It may be included in a monthly newsletter or distributed door to door by community volunteers.

## Financial Planning

The board or community manager should review each event and decide how much to allocate—if anything—in the budget. It's important that event planning is coordinated with the annual budget development to ensure that the necessary funds are available.

## A Happy Ending

Community spirit has returned and the community has evolved into a new phase since we re-evaluated our programs. Residents are once again interacting, learning, and sharing with each other. They're socializing with each other, providing a network and support system for other residents, and taking care of each other. They've redefined socialization and the programs that promote it, they've re-organized the social committee and expanded its purpose, and they've created a new sense of pride and purpose in the community.

As management professionals we stopped to re-examine actions and activities that we had often taken at face value; and, in the act of challenging ourselves, we challenged our community. Together, management and the board successfully updated our focus, and in the process improved the quality of life for residents. Once again, we are a community.

Although not all of these programs are appropriate for every community association, this is a list of perennially popular programs for all types of community associations.

**WINTER PARTY/TEEN NIGHT/SWEETHEARTS DANCE** Ask the community if there is a budding DJ or secure the services of a professional DJ to play music for an evening. This is popular with teens between 13 and 16. The event is best run on a Friday night between the hours of 8:00 p.m. and 10:00 p.m., and requires the assistance of approximately one adult for every 10 teens. The association can order pizza and soda or other convenient food. A modest cover charge (for example, $2.00 per teen) will offset some of the cost, but overcharging could make the party unaffordable for some resident teens.

*Requires: Clubhouse or public square, music, food, and adult supervision.*

**SUMMER PICNIC/4TH OF JULY PARTY/BLOCK PARTY** A great meet-your-neighbor event, outdoor parties are appropriate where no club house is available. Any occasion will do: the opening or closing of the community pool, holidays like the 4th of July or Labor Day, or your own community's Association Day. Generally a hot dog and hamburger style cook out works well. The association should supply the grills, charcoal, hot dogs and hamburgers, rolls, and condiments. Ask homeowners to bring their own beverage and side dishes. You can make the entrance fee a bottle of soda, a covered dish, a jumbo size bag of chips, or a dessert.

*Requires: Volunteers to set up, cook, and clean up; paper goods.*

**EASTER EGG HUNT** Plastic eggs are filled with tickets redeemable for prizes and candy, and the eggs are placed in a section of the common ground. This is an event for children about two to five. Older children can be guides who help younger ones find and collect the eggs. The guides are rewarded with chocolate bunnies or special gifts that are age appropriate. After all the eggs are collected and the tickets are redeemed for prizes and candy, it can be fun to serve hot chocolate and cookies. This event is best run between 10:00 a.m. noon. (Set a rain date as well.)

*Requires: Open space, several dozen plastic eggs, lots of jellybeans and other wrapped candy, chocolate bunnies, prizes, hot chocolate, and cookies.*

**HALLOWEEN PARADE** Residents (adults too!) dress in costumes and parade through the community. Ask for a volunteer to take pictures of each participant and to ensure that everyone receives a copy of his or her picture. This should be a late morning event on a Saturday that culminates in a picnic on the common grounds. Provide trick-or-treat bags, pizza, donuts and cider, or juice or a warm drink. Make the event more festive by playing Halloween music during the picnic.

*Requires: Open space, music, camera and film, trick-or-treat bags, food if desired, and adult supervision.*

**VISIT FROM SANTA** This requires a fair amount of coordination, but only one volunteer to dress as Santa and deliver presents to children in the community on a pre-arranged evening. Parents purchase and wrap each gift. They also tag each gift with the name and address where the gift should be delivered and drop it off at Santa's house in advance. Santa begins his rounds at 6:00 p.m. He doesn't enter the house, or he'll be late for his other deliveries! Remember, this all happens in *one night.*

*Requires: one very dedicated volunteer, and a Santa suit.*

**ADOPT A CHARITY/FOOD DRIVE** Many charities will welcome gifts from community food drives throughout the year. It's easiest to have homeowners leave their donation on their doorstep on an arranged date and time. If there is a Boy Scout or Girl Scout troop in your area, this is a great way for them to earn their community service badges. The volunteers in the community pick up the donations from each doorstep and deliver them to the local food shelter. Canned goods, boxed goods such as cereal, rice, pasta, and cleaning supplies or paper goods are always needed.

*Requires: volunteers to pick up and deliver the donations.*

**MY PERSPECTIVE**

**Jo-Ann M. Greenstein** is with Advantage Property Management in Morganville, NJ.

*Community spirit can be built—and rebuilt. To do so simply requires an honest look at how to best connect with the people in the community. Are there more children? Retirees? Singles? Widowers? Working families? Take a look and then think about what they want from a community. Weekend activities? Nighttime functions? Sedate functions? There may be a place for all of these, or just a few.*

# CHAPTER
# 5

*By Drew Mulhare,*
CMCA, AMS, LSM, PCAM

# Community Spirit
*How to Gain and Maintain Momentum*

As an association manager, I've been extremely fortunate to work in a community whose residents are generally happy, helpful, and involved. Of course, there are occasions where neighbor-to-neighbor disputes need mitigating, contractors aren't fulfilling all of their obligations, and I must work to achieve quorums at a meeting. But, for the most part, the spirit of the community remains high. What is the secret to this success? Momentum. Much like the saying, "the hardest million dollars to make is the first million," the most challenging part of promoting community spirit is generating it to begin with.

Fostering enthusiasm for our community begins with the manager and the board, but will ultimately fail unless we include the residents. The task involves—but is so much more than—cheerleading, smiling, and saying "good job!" when things are going well. Every aspect of the association's business functions, governance, and social agenda is approached with a determination to achieve resident satisfaction. It works.

Of the various roles
community associations
play, perhaps the
most important, yet
also most elusive
and difficult to define
is its social role.

My community is a great example of how the correct attitudes, mentalities, and enthusiasm tend to remain afloat—once they are in place—with a reasonable amount of guidance and oversight.

In order to define community spirit and identify the association's role in putting the community first, association leaders should continually ask fundamental questions to determine and update their business model and strategic plan. Why do people choose to live in your community? What lead to their decision to reside here, and are their initial expectations being met or exceeded? Are people generally moving in, or are they trying to get out to another comparable community in your region? Are the members (as customers) satisfied with the maintenance, recreation, and perhaps security that the association, as a business, is providing? What can the association do to improve its relationships with its customers and maximize their social experience?

## The Association's Role

Of the various roles community associations play, perhaps the most important, yet also most elusive and difficult to define is its social role. Though distinct, it's an integral part of the business and governance roles of the association, and the success of the community relies on it for balance in customer satisfaction, effective management, and efficient operations. A successful social program promotes contented members, indicated by prompt payment of assessments and routine compliance with reasonable rules.

How a community lives may be reflected in how it looks. What indicates that residents enjoy living in your community and are involved in its daily rhythm? Is the community welcoming and are people smiling? Are people volunteering and serving their neighbors? Is the social calendar full of activities that address a variety of interests? Does the association invite newcomers to events designed to welcome and integrate them into the community as quickly as possible? Is the monthly newsletter fun, engaging, and positive?

What makes a community an enjoyable place to live? It starts with enthusiastic people who are interested in making their community the best it can be. These are people who enjoy fun and make it contagious. People who are unafraid of failure,

A highly functional community of neighbors sharing interests and resources speaks to all the human needs described by Abraham Maslow in the middle of the 20th century. Perhaps that's why community associations are so important in today's lifestyles.

Maslow was a social psychologist who identified a hierarchy of human needs. The most basic is physiological: the need for air, water, food, sleep, and shelter. Shelter is, of course, a typical function in a community association.

Next in the hierarchy is safety, defined as stability and consistency in a chaotic world. Associations provide physical safety through the close proximity of neighbors, by maintaining a reasonably secure environment, and possibly by using security equipment or trained personnel. They also provide psychological safety by establishing and enforcing policies that ensure stability and consistency within the community.

According to Maslow, the need for love comes next. It's defined as the desire to belong to groups and the need to be needed. A community association is certainly a group where people are needed and that provides camaraderie, social activities, special interest clubs, and committee and board members opportunities.

After the need for love, people need esteem; they need to feel competent at their tasks and to receive attention and recognition. Community associations provide many opportunities for people to earn esteem. Residents can serve on committees and boards, organize and host events, contribute to the newsletter or website, or advocate for community concerns with local and state governments. The association also provides esteem to members by publicly recognizing outstanding volunteerism.

After all their other needs have been met, people finally feel a need to grow. Maslow divided this need into the need for self-actualization (defined as self-fulfillment and realizing one's potential) and transcendence (the need to help others find fulfillment and reach their potential). Association residents find self-actualization and transcendence in the many volunteer and charitable functions and activities both within and outside of the community; and many realize their true potential when they become community leaders.

Your community may transcend by simply welcoming new residents or conducting food and clothing drives throughout the year. Communities that directly assist those in need through caring neighbor programs, support schools and youth programs, interact with government officials, participate in municipal outreach programs, and provide material and monetary value to local charities have achieved highly developed transcendence.

willing to try new ideas, invest time, support others, see that there's always more than one way to accomplish goals, and facilitate other peoples' success.

Across the country, many small associations run entirely by volunteers and large associations that are professionally managed provide examples of successful programs that promote community spirit. Some of these are reflected in *Best Practices in Community Harmony/Spirit/Involvement*, a report prepared by the Foundation for Community Association Research in 2001 (available at www.cairf.org/research/bp.html).

The key to these successful practices isn't the size or wealth of the association—rather it's the energy of the association's people. These are people who see the need and are willing to step up and engage in the process; people who'll apply the same energy to help their neighbors as to help their best friend. It takes people who are unwilling to allow the same volunteers to always shoulder the burden for the entire group and eventually burn out. It takes people willing to nurture an idea and then give it to others to improve upon in future opportunities. It takes people who consider the social needs of the association to be as important as the business and governance of the association.

The leaders must prioritize funding and opportunities for its social mission. The business managers of the association must realize that, just as marketing drives sales, social excellence drives the business and governance roles of the association. Without an attractive and engaging lifestyle, there will soon be little business to conduct and few to govern.

## The Manager's Roles

### Prioritizer

I believe a vital part of a manager's role is recognizing that the social aspect of association business is a priority and conveying that to the board. Part of that role is to help the board understand the relationship between socially engaged neighbors and increased participation and assistance in the business and governance of the association. When a manager recommends a budget to the board it should specifically allocate funds for social opportunities thus making them a priority.

### Cheerleader

Start the spark and fan the flame as necessary, but make sure everyone else glows in the warmth of appreciation and recognition. Congratulate and recognize volunteers as often as possible and more than necessary. They'll be shy and embarrassed, but also very grateful and fulfilled. Use the newsletter and annual meeting to showcase and thank specific volunteers for their time and talents in making their community special. Communicate plans and ideas at each opportunity and venue to increase participation. Actively encourage the board to enable volunteers to participate in the social agenda.

### Observer

The manager should be aware of the people in the community that tend to be starters and organizers. Know the people the community can go to for special event programming and brain storming ideas. Create a resource by keeping notes of residents' and volunteers' special interests and talents.

### Bystander

Leave the social programs to the volunteers. When a manager organizes a program or hosts an event, it tends to be too commercial. Besides, friends socializing and planning among friends always have more fun. Imperfection is part of the design. They'll enjoy it more if they do it themselves.

### Committee Liaison

Encourage the board to appoint a social committee and to fill it with dedicated, active, fun people. As manager, your role will be to guide and support them. They should create a calendar of events; keep notes of what has worked and why; and, as importantly, what didn't work and why. A manager's role is also to be a resource when the committee needs assistance with special events or support for new ideas. Have the committee draft an "after-action" report, and file it for future use in budgeting, lessons learned, and contacts.

### Press Agent

Another role for the manager is publicizing the social nature of the community—within the association and to the local community. Draft press releases about upcoming or particularly successful events and send them to the local papers in addition to your association newsletter. Take pictures and send them along with the release. (Remember to thank everyone at every opportunity.)

### Scheduler

The manager should keep an eye on the social calendar and fill in blank spots. Look forward on the calendar and plan for special events. For example, ask the landscaping committee in January to work with the social committee to begin planning the annual Arbor Day celebration.

### Pollster

Even great social programs will fail if residents aren't interested. Managers should survey residents and base the association's social agenda on their interests. Resident feedback is very important to keep the social agenda meaningful and exciting.

## The Board's Roles

### Business Managers

The most significant breakthrough for a board comes when they understand that they're the principal operators in a local business. Much more than just giving some time to their community because it is the right thing to do, the board is operating a business. The association's business products and services are community lifestyle and facilities maintenance. The board is elected to preserve, protect, and enhance not only the common property, but also the community lifestyle. Unfortunately, association governing documents, especially the older ones, don't adequately address social needs as a business function. In fact, most documents would classify the social aspect as discretionary, while insurance, physical asset maintenance, and replacement reserves are typically listed as required elements.

### Visionaries

As business managers, the board must be more visionary than bylaws and CC&Rs require. Board members must ask themselves: Do we realize that a key aspect of protecting and enhancing the value of the common property is whether people actually want to live in our community? What is the quality of our product? How do we stay ahead of competitors in offering better products and services? Do our customers refer our community to others? What personnel, programming, and financial resources do we commit to preserving and enhancing our lifestyle?

### Investors
Since quality of life is part of the mission of the community, boards should understand that it's good business to make it a priority. The return on this investment is significant in communities whose neighborhood lifestyle includes community excitement. Boards also need to recognize that they must allocate resources just as they would for any other business objective.

In community associations, boards must communicate the mission, create reasonable budgets that enable goals, encourage volunteers to work and residents to participate. Get the right people involved and support them. Solicit new ideas and encourage idea makers to become solution contributors. Create a community theme. Create a community mission statement. Adopt special events as signatures for your community.

## The Residents' Roles

### Participants
Since residents aren't required to follow any strategic plan or job description, how can they create community spirit? Their role is to catch the spirit, and they will, once awakened by positive, subtle peer-pressure.

Residents aren't required to improve their community beyond adhering to the aesthetic and behavioral standards outlined in the association's governing documents. However, restraining oneself from staking a pink flamingo in the front yard does not constitute community spirit. Still, residents in communities with a strong positive spirit tend to adhere to the community standards more readily (knowingly or unknowingly) and volunteer their time and talents to promote neighborhood camaraderie.

### Thrifties
Some residents feel they pay too much in fees already and costly social events may cause animosity. Many successful community

spirit programs cost little, and still generate plenty of good will and neighborliness. Therefore, keeping costs low for some programs may be important.

### Hosts

Some of the best community spirit programs rise from the immediate neighborhood level up to the association level. Neighbors should host block parties at least once a year, and should be the first to welcome newcomers to the street. True, many events can be generated by the board or a manager, but top down programs can be difficult to sustain in the long term. Boards and managers must keep their ears to the ground, and support whatever is already going on in the community.

**MY PERSPECTIVE**

**Drew Mulhare** is Vice President of Realtec Community Services in Williamsburg, Virginia.

*Throughout this chapter you've read the word people many times. It should be obvious that people are the key to achieving community spirit. This doesn't mean only people on the board. It doesn't mean a small handful of residents. It means all types of residents must be inspired to join in the association's affairs, since it's fun, rewarding, and because their neighbors are involved as well.*

*Building community spirit can be hard work, since it may require changing people's attitudes and creating a good buzz in the streets. But, I've seen how positive momentum can turn would-be indifferent residents into contributing members of the community. I believe that most people want to live in a place that is fun and friendly, and that they can be proud of. Playing to those qualities is the start of building spirit in any place. Try it. You'll be happy with the result!*

*By Ronald L. Perl, ESQ.*

# Model Governance
## How to Create the Ideal Framework for Your Community Association

The president of a condominium association had recently breached his ethical obligations by engaging in self-dealing and the community was in turmoil. Apparently he owned an undisclosed interest in both the community association's landscaping and maintenance companies, and they were charging higher than market rates for their services. As details emerged, so did the gossip among the neighbors. Soon, residents were talking of recall elections and legal action, and a dark cloud hung over the community. Ultimately, the president—and four other board members who had rubber-stamped his actions—resigned.

The two remaining board members, once considered dissenters by the former president, and three new appointees comprised the new board. This group recognized that to regain the trust and confidence of the community, and to prevent such unethical action in the future, they'd need to create a completely new governance structure. The new board's first step was to fire the on-site manager—who had known about the former president's self-dealing. Based on a strong recommendation from a neighboring community, the association retained a reputable, professional management company. Together, they rebuilt the community from scratch.

## What is Model Governance?

Model governance is a term used to describe the optimal structure for governing a community association. It outlines reasonable procedures that empower boards and staff to perform efficiently, taking into account the rights of individual owners to privacy, to enjoy their homes, and to participate in the community association.

Community associations are often described as having three core functions: governance, business, and social. These three functions are interdependent; each relies on the success of the other two for a balance of satisfied residents, effective management, and efficient operations.

Model governance encompasses the typical governing functions—meetings, elections, and rules development and enforcement—but that doesn't exclude other functions. It's a term that describes the ideal governance framework—one that recognizes the business and community functions of the association, encourages strategic and visionary leadership, includes *all* association members, and results in strong, vibrant, and harmonious community associations.

Too often, community association boards rework tired ideas, engage in trivial matters, and fail to act as a group. In short, they're usually criticized for one of two reasons—they're not involved enough or they're too involved. In reality, boards should be more engaged in some things and less in others. No one will argue that ideally boards should *govern*, rather than get caught up in non-essential matters.

However, board members, like everyone else, tend to lead busy lives, requiring that they make good use of the time, energy, and wisdom spent on association issues. Boards who adhere to model governance structures and standards will get the best return on their effort and achieve their desired results. Community associations need a model—not merely anecdotal wisdom—

to help a board and manager know when and how to get involved and when to just leave things alone.

No matter how dedicated or intelligent the individuals may be, community associations and their residents cannot maximize their potential in a poorly designed system.

## Basic Structure

The new board thought it would be good to review the roles, rights, and responsibilities of the board and the association members. This analysis would allow them to delineate board functions from member functions and demonstrate the importance of the entire community engaging in the association's daily functioning.

They turned to the Community Associations Institute and used its "Rights and Responsibilities for Better Communities: Principles for Homeowners and Community Leaders" as their guide. This document gave them a stronger feel for the various roles and functions of the association members and board, and they forged ahead in their reconstruction effort. They now focused on examining their governing documents. They found that their association's documents were pretty typical: A five-member board governed the community; the board elected its officers—president, vice president, secretary, and treasurer; the board had the authority to establish committees; and a covenants committee existed as a standing committee.

## Creating Committees

The new board knew it would be important to involve as many residents in the rebuilding process as possible. Therefore, they put out a call for volunteers to owners and tenants alike for a number of new committees: buildings and grounds, finance, recreation and social, and for the existing covenants committee.

The buildings and grounds committee assists the board and manager to review proposals for landscaping and building maintenance contracts, review the contractor's work in those areas, and recommends physical enhancements.

The finance committee works with the association's treasurer and manager to track expenses, delinquencies, and income. It also helps draft the association's budget and long-range financial plan.

The recreation and social committee coordinates and plans social activities for both adults and children, and supervises pool and tennis court operations.

The covenants committee provides internal conflict resolution, mediation, and arbitration for owner disputes and rules infractions.

The board made it clear to the residents that these committees would have substantial responsibility and that the board would be guided by their recommendations. The committees would make recommendations to the board on key issues including setting policy, selecting contractors, spending association funds, and other related issues.

## Adopting a Code of Ethics

The board determined that it should operate under a code of ethics, which it developed based on the advice of the association attorney. The new code prohibited the association from contracting with any board member or any entity in which a board member had an ownership interest.

The typical code of ethics only requires disclosure and consent of the disinterested board members, but this board wanted to go one step further in light of its recent incident. The board determined that there were enough vendors in every category that the association wouldn't suffer if board members or their related entities were eliminated. At the same time, the board demanded that its management company disclose in detail all transactions it had with related entities and any and all compensation offered to the company's managers.

## Reviewing the Rules

The association had never reviewed the rules originally put in place by the developer. Some rules made no sense, some rules hadn't been enforced in years, and some previously unknown rules surprised the new board members. Rules had been enforced sporadically at best, based on the whims of the former president. The association attorney advised the board that governing well requires that they re-examine the rules continually. A well-run association should have no more rules than are absolutely necessary to protect the residents and preserve the property.

The board appointed a task force to look at all the rules, determine which were necessary, and identify those needing revision. The board asked the task force to present their recommendations to the residents at an open meeting.

An association member who was an attorney lead the task force. That added some expertise and strength to the group, but it wasn't required to perform this job. The task force developed revised rules and discussed them with the board and the association's attorney. They prepared a final draft based on the feedback they collected, circulated it to the association members, and asked them to respond with written suggestions.

The board scheduled an open meeting for all residents, including tenants, at which the task force presented its recommendations. Attendees made additional comments. The task force reviewed all comments and made a final recommendation to the board. The board adopted an updated set of rules and regulations that was the product of the entire community's participation.

## Resolving Conflict

The board understood that, despite attempts to enact rules acceptable to the members, conflicts would arise. To resolve conflicts and avoid unnecessary litigation, the board would use alternative dispute resolution (ADR).

The board felt that many rules were broken because members weren't familiar with the governing documents. Therefore, the association adopted a progressive approach to conflict resolution, beginning with a friendly telephone call from the manager, which the board believed would prevent minor issues from escalating and creating ill will.

After the phone call, the association next sent a friendly, non-confrontational letter that described the alleged problem and suggested that, if true, it might conflict with an association rule. The letter encouraged the resident to call the manager to resolve the issue. If neither the call nor the letter worked, the manager sent a series of notices that put the resident on notice and provided an opportunity for ADR.

Covenants committee members, who had been trained in basic mediation techniques by the association's attorney, would mediate owner disputes. These volunteers were able to resolve

**Homeowners Have the Right To:**

1. A responsive and competent community association.

2. Honest, fair and respectful treatment by community leaders and managers.

3. Participate in governing the community association by attending meetings, serving on committees and standing for election.

4. Access appropriate association books and records.

5. Prudent expenditure of fees and other assessments.

6. Live in a community where the property is maintained according to established standards.

7. Fair treatment regarding financial and other association obligations, including the opportunity to discuss payment plans and options with the association before foreclosure is initiated.

8. Receive all documents that address rules and regulations governing the community association—if not prior to purchase and settlement by a real estate agent or attorney, then upon joining the community.

9. Appeal to appropriate community leaders those decisions affecting non-routine financial responsibilities or property rights.

**Homeowners Have
the Responsibility To:**

1. Read and comply with the governing documents of the community.

2. Maintain their property according to established standards.

3. Treat association leaders honestly and with respect.

4. Vote in community elections and on other issues.

5. Pay association assessments and charges on time.

6. Contact association leaders or managers, if necessary, to discuss financial obligations and alternative payment arrangements.

7. Request reconsideration of material decisions that personally affect them.

8. Provide current contact information to association leaders or managers to help ensure they receive information from the community.

9. Ensure that those who reside on their property (e.g., tenants, relatives, friends) adhere to all rules and regulations.

**Community Leaders Have
the Right To:**

1. Expect owners and non-owner residents to meet their financial obligations to the community.

2. Expect residents to know and comply with the rules and regulations of the community and to stay informed by reading materials provided by the association.

3. Respectful and honest treatment from residents.

4. Conduct meetings in a positive and constructive atmosphere.

5. Receive support and constructive input from owners and non-owner residents.

6. Personal privacy at home and during leisure time in the community.

7. Take advantage of educational opportunities (e.g., publications, training workshops) that are directly related to their responsibilities, and as approved by the association.

## Community Leaders Have the Responsibility To:

1. Fulfill their fiduciary duties to the community and exercise discretion in a manner they reasonably believe to be in the best interests of the community.

2. Exercise sound business judgment and follow established management practices.

3. Balance the needs and obligations of the community as a whole with those of individual homeowners and residents.

4. Understand the association's governing documents and become educated with respect to applicable state and local laws, and to manage the community association accordingly.

5. Establish committees or use other methods to obtain input from owners and non-owner residents.

6. Conduct open, fair and well-publicized elections.

7. Welcome and educate new members of the community—owners and non-owner residents alike.

8. Encourage input from residents on issues affecting them personally and the community as a whole.

9. Encourage events that foster neighborliness and a sense of community.

10. Conduct business in a transparent manner when feasible and appropriate.

11. Allow homeowners access to appropriate community records, when requested.

12. Collect all monies due from owners and non-owner residents.

13. Devise appropriate and reasonable arrangements, when needed and as feasible, to facilitate the ability of individual homeowners to meet their financial obligations to the community.

14. Provide a process that residents can use to appeal decisions affecting their non-routine financial responsibilities or property rights—where permitted by law and the association's governing documents.

15. Initiate foreclosure proceedings only as a measure of last resort.

16. Make covenants, conditions and restrictions as understandable as possible, adding clarifying lay language or supplementary materials when drafting or revising the documents.

17. Provide complete and timely disclosure of personal and financial conflicts of interest related to the actions of community leaders, e.g., officers, the board and committees.

To resolve conflicts
and avoid unnecessary
litigation, the board
would use alternative
dispute resolution.

many resident disputes that the association had faced in the past and expected in the future. The covenants committee also would investigate complaints of rules violations brought either by the association or by residents.

## Board Meetings

The previous board hadn't held regular meetings; but, the new board decided not only to conduct regular monthly meetings, but to open all meetings to the members. The only matters they would discuss in executive session would be those requiring confidentiality, such as pending litigation or contract negotiations. The new board would vote, make financial decisions, adopt rules, and handle almost all association business in open meetings.

The board now also conducted its work sessions in the presence of residents. The board hoped this would restore the trust destroyed by the prior administration. Owners and residents now felt connected to their association; and, this, in turn, encouraged greater participation.

## Membership Meetings

To increase member participation and keep members informed, the board scheduled quarterly membership meetings—the annual meeting, a budget forum, and two general meetings.

The new open governance structure was well-received. At first, members used the new forum to express anger and frustration over the former board's practices. However, the owners quickly understood that changes had been made.

The association distributed meeting agendas before and minutes after each meeting. Even those who couldn't attend were informed about association operations. The association circulated draft budgets before the budget forum, ensuring that owners had an opportunity to study the budget and participate in the meeting intelligently. Everyone found it helpful when owners understood association finances.

The association held open elections in which no association member was related in any way to a board member or candidate. With management's guidance, they conducted an open, self-nomination process, controlled the proxy process independent

of the board, distributed candidate biographies fairly, and counted ballots in the presence of representatives of all candidates.

The association held general meetings solely to inform residents and to provide owners with an open forum.

As a result of all of this, the association eliminated distrust and
the them-vs.-us mentality. More owners began to participate,
and it became easier for the association to create consensus, even
on difficult issues.

## MY PERSPECTIVE

**Ronald L. Perl** is an
association attorney
with Hill-Wallack in
Princeton, New Jersey.

*There's no single governance structure that will work for every association.
There are, however, some principles that are common to successful models.
First, there must be openness. For any society or sub-society to function
harmoniously, governance must be in the open to avoid distrust and
allow the stakeholders to be informed. Second, owners have the right to
determine their direction and to define the common good. Involvement
and participation are keys to a successful community association.
Participation makes a governing board stronger, not weaker. Third, the
governance and business functions of community associations must
always be viewed in the context of community. Community is what
distinguishes governance of a common interest community from govern-
mental agencies.*

# 7

*By Lucia Anna Trigiani,*
*ESQ.*

# Good Rules

## *How They Promote Community Spirit*

A few years ago, I had an epiphany about association rules when I found myself in the middle of a fairly well publicized issue for one of my clients in Virginia. The case arose out of a basic architectural enforcement matter. The association had approved an application for a resident owner to build a tree house for his daughter. However, the tree house that was constructed was *substantially* different from the approved application. Neighbors complained. Over the next six months, the association made numerous attempts to work with the homeowner to coordinate the removal of the tree house.

Eventually, the case caught the attention of the national media —the association president was on the morning news, and the Associated Press picked up the story. This attention snowballed into quite a media event. Hate mail arrived from an international tree-house support group, and "Save the Tree House" tee shirts were suddenly available at the local shopping center.

The stories didn't report the good news about how the board handled itself—the efforts they made to work with the tree house owners. The board attempted to resolve the issue with the homeowner before taking legal action. In spite of those efforts, the homeowner took the issue public and set off a media circus. Through it all, the board maintained its composure, due in great part to the strong leadership of the association president.

What I remember most about the tree house case—and what was eye opening for me—wasn't the attack on the board and the association for enforcing rules. Rather, I was inspired by the phenomenal support the board received from community members. This was most evident when a substantial majority of homeowners appeared at a public meeting, where the board expected to be lynched. Speaker after speaker rose in support of the board to voice their agreement with the board's efforts to protect the rules.

That's when it became clear to me that the silent majority of homeowners in community associations supports rules—when they're created and enforced reasonably. Good rules are an essential component for achieving and maintaining community. Community association boards must listen to their constituents, the silent as well as the noisy, and stand behind their decisions in developing and enforcing rules.

## Reasonable Rules Make Great Communities

A community association's approach to rules is a critical element in creating, maintaining, and promoting community. The process of making and amending rules speaks volumes about the association, sets the tone for the community, and is an integral part of turning homeowners into neighbors. Reasonable rules, when fairly and uniformly enforced, can be the most important asset to a community. They provide sought after structure to the community, can help prevent neighbor-to-neighbor feuds, and make good business sense.

Unfortunately, rules and their enforcement often invite negative press—usually when association actions are misunderstood. But, when rules are unreasonable or enforcement is mean-spirited, the press will find and report the story.

- Rules must be enacted and enforced uniformly, taking into account the consequences.

- Developing rules for the sake of having rules is an unnecessary exercise. Develop a rule only if it is necessary.

- Rules must be based on proper authority.

- Rules shouldn't be about unreasonably limiting activities of residents or punishing a specific neighbor. Instead, rules must be about protecting a resident's ability to enjoy the community and protecting the value of property from disruptive or harmful behavior of others.

- The focus of rules should be to encourage understanding and compliance.

## How to Craft a Reasonable Rule

The first question an association should ask when considering new rules or amending existing rules should be, "Do we really need a rule?" If the answer is Yes, then craft rules that are positive, easy to understand, and that let residents know exactly what will happen if the rule isn't followed. Residents must know what's expected, and a well-drafted rule is the starting point.

### Be Plain and Brief

If community association rules are cumbersome, residents won't read them, much less follow them. It's important, therefore, to state a rule in plain language, keep it brief, and be specific.

### Be Positive

Compliance with rules is easier for residents if the rules specify correct behavior rather than just state what isn't permitted. Whenever possible, state rules in positive language. Otherwise, add information about what to do instead.

### Include the Reason

People tend to ignore or dismiss what they don't understand. Rules that seem unnecessary or gratuitous will usually be ignored and may be difficult to enforce. Therefore, providing a brief explanation of the rule can contribute to compliance.

"
**The rule adoption
process may be
as important
as the rule itself.**

### State the Consequences

People are motivated to abide by rules when they have an appreciation of the consequences. Include information about what a resident can expect if the rules aren't followed.

## How to Adopt a New Rule

The rule adoption process may be as important as the rule itself. In some states, if the correct process isn't followed, the rule is invalid. Be sure to investigate local laws or ask a professional community association manager or experienced community association attorney for assistance.

After the proposed rule is crafted, distribute it using the association newsletter, bulletin boards, or website. Conduct public meetings or allow for public comment periods during board meetings to discuss the need for the rule with residents and invite them to comment on the proposal. Allow adequate time for community members to comment, and don't rely on one means of communication—not every one will visit the website or attend a board meeting. Consider homeowner feedback carefully and revise the draft appropriately.

Once the rule is finalized, the board must formally adopt it at a properly convened board meeting to avoid legal challenges. Record the adoption in the meeting minutes as evidence of formal adoption and to assure successful enforcement. Once adopted, distribute the rule to owners and residents and include updated rules in resale disclosure documents.

## Conduct a Rules Audit

Occasionally associations should examine their rules and ask, "Do we need this rule?" "Is this rule still legal and valid?" and be prepared to revise obsolete rules. For example, the Telecommunications Act of 1996 compelled community associations to revise rules on satellite dishes.

One of the benefits of a rules audit is that raising questions about rules can create dialog among owners and residents. Rule changes can elicit reaction; and, homeowners will buy into rules that they've developed or changed.

## STEPS FOR ADOPTING A RULE

- Develop a draft rule

- Distribute the draft rule to residents and owners

- Invite resident feedback

- Consider residents' comments

- Revise the rule as appropriate

- Adopt the rule formally

- Publish the rule

## Gentle Reminders

Even owners who have actually read the rules will need a reminder from time to time, and there are a number of ways to continuously educate residents about them:

**Newsletters.** Create a "Rule Reminder" or "Our Neighborhood" column in your newsletter to highlight a specific rule, ask for feedback about a rule, or explain a rule that's been overlooked.

**Signs.** Whether the problem is related to parking, trash collection, or use of common areas, the association can post rules creatively and permanently using signs—Permit Parking Only, Rules of the Pool, and others provide constant reminders.

**Websites.** All information about your rules—the resale package, resident handbook, newsletter articles, or policies—can and should be placed on your website. Make them easy to find.

Be creative when getting the word out—think of absurd examples that will stick with the residents. Or, try to touch the homeowners with real life examples.

## Achieving Community Buy-In

The final goal of the association is achieving compliance with the rules by all residents. Enforcement isn't about punishment, it's about compliance. This was the key to the stability of the community with the tree house. They knew that compliance requires common sense, creativity, patience, flexibility, and consistency; and, the association only got involved when the rule was clearly violated.

As a first step, associations should try an informal approach to gain voluntary compliance to rules. Informal efforts can avoid expensive litigation, and may be received as more neighborly. Start slow and easy, and ramp up efforts as needed. There are a few simple steps to encourage voluntary compliance and eliminate problems before formal measures become necessary.

### Personal Contact

When problems arise, start with simple personal contact. Particularly in small communities, a phone call or a knock on the door with a friendly reminder and an appeal for compliance may be all that's needed. Personal contact promotes a sense of community and fosters cooperation among residents who will see managers and board members as caring neighbors rather than enforcers.

### The First Written Notice

When you need to notify a resident through the mail, start with a friendly, polite letter explaining the violation. It's important to be positive and allow the resident the benefit of the doubt. Personalize form letters and use a casual tone. A firmer, more serious tone can be saved for a second or third notice. Of course, send thank you notes to residents who correct violations.

### Exceptions and Consistency

Occasionally, an association will discover an unusual situation or unique problem that begs for an exception to a rule. Making exceptions may weaken rules—something boards are naturally reluctant to do. But failing to make an exception—under exceptional circumstances—isn't the way to be reasonable.

Sometimes *not* making an exception results in greater harm to the community. Consider the case of six-year-old leukemia patient Brage Sassin of Tampa, Florida. His parents built a tree house that stood six feet higher than allowed. When the association ordered the Sassin's to remove the tree house, the media outcry was widespread and brutal. An exception in this case, wouldn't have resulted in a proliferation of high-rise tree houses throughout the community. The Tampa Palms Association found a creative solution by asking for a doctor's note confirming that the tree house was a medical necessity.

Similarly, keep in mind that laws intended to prevent discrimination like the Fair Housing Act may require associations to offer reasonable accommodations to residents in the form of an exception to a rule. One common accommodation is making exceptions to the pet rules to allow service animals in a no-pet community.

Exceptions should be rare, but not unheard of. For all other violations, consistency is essential to success. In addition to meeting the legal obligation to enforce rules uniformly, the board should also meet its obligation to the community to promote harmony and community spirit. And, on those occasions when the law says that accommodations must be made, make them. Inconsistent enforcement practices invariably divide residents and promote discord.

### The Grace Period

If you're enacting a new rule, amending an old one, or just beefing up your compliance efforts, give residents time to adjust. For some, compliance might require some creative problem solving, and that can take a little time. Set your implementation date far enough in the future that the association has adequate time to notify all residents—repeatedly—of the change, and they have adequate time to make it. After the rule goes into effect, set aside a time (30, 60, 90 days) where only warnings are issued.

### The Grandfather Clause

Consider the effect of new rules on current residents. Grandfather clauses are a reasonable way to address concerns of residents who selected a home in your association based on certain expectations—that they could have pets or park a pickup truck in the driveway. Grandfather clauses can also make maintaining harmony a challenge. New residents may be confused or resentful when they have to comply with a rule that their neighbor doesn't. An ongoing education campaign will be needed so that everyone understands the reasons for the different treatment.

## Formal Enforcement

Sometimes friendly, informal methods to gain compliance with rules just don't get results, and more formal means must be used. Getting formal means using certain procedures—called due process—that must be followed to protect the rights of the residents and the association.

### Due Process

Due process is a legal term that translates simply to basic fairness. The person who is alleged to have violated a rule must be treated fairly and afforded basic rights. Develop a standard due process procedure and apply it consistently. This procedure is itself a rule and should be reasonable and adopted after public comment.

### The Essentials of Due Process

The essential elements of the association's due process must be part of the rule enforcement procedure. These essentials are notice, opportunity for hearing, and the opportunity to be represented by legal counsel.

Formally notifying a resident of an alleged violation is the first step in due process. The notice must contain certain information:

■ A description of the alleged rule violation.

■ A restatement of the rule.

■ The possible penalty.

■ Specific corrective action by the resident by a specific date.

■ Action that may be taken if the violation isn't corrected by the deadline.

■ Information about the opportunity to offer a defense against the charge (hearing).

Before you impose a penalty, the association must conduct a hearing to consider evidence of a violation and to provide the owner the opportunity to offer a defense against the charge. When violations are based on a resident's complaint, be sure to verify the situation. Also, provide for an appeals process as part of your procedures.

## Monetary Charges and Penalties

What happens when the association and the resident have concluded the hearing and yet remain in opposition? What steps should be taken next to gain compliance? The association can impose monetary penalties—which work very well with some residents—or the association may suspend privileges for those who don't respond when hit in the wallet.

Some state statutes and association governing documents grant authority to community associations to impose monetary charges (fines) for rules violations.

Local laws and sometimes governing documents allow community associations to suspend an owner's voting privileges or right to use facilities or services, as long as they have access to their property and their health, safety, or property isn't endangered.

Suspending privileges has a more immediate effect than imposing fines. The inconvenience caused by having a parking pass revoked may motivate residents to resolve the situation. The resident who can ignore a monetary penalty will find it much harder to ignore that the cable has been cut off. Before taking away a resident's privileges, be sure that the association adopts a policy resolution expressly enacting the power to suspend privileges.

## MY PERSPECTIVE

**Lucia Anna Trigiani** is an attorney with Troutman Sanders in McLean, Virginia.

*We all cringe at the thought of seeing our community association featured on the nightly news or in a print exposé as the oppressive community association plaguing the disenfranchised homeowner. Perhaps we're all just one bad decision away from being that community. Sure, rules are restrictive and based on something negative—bad behavior. As I tell community association leaders who encounter rule violations with some frequency: it's all about bad manners, isn't it?*

*But, as my experience in the tree house story reveals, sometimes the whole story isn't told when it makes the news—facts just don't make good news stories.*

*The real news story should be about how rules protect and preserve communities. Associations that have reasonable enforcement practices, inclusive rule adoption methods, and attention to the people-side of rules compliance are successful communities that protect assets and promote community. Rules are both a sword and a shield for building and maintaining community.*

**CHAPTER**

# 8

*By Beth A. Grimm,*
*ESQ.*

# Alternative Dispute Resolution

*How Mediation Solved a Tough Problem and Saved $50,000*

Unsavory-looking kids had overrun the park in a medium-sized homeowner association, and some thought they were members of a gang. Most of them hung out with the teenage sons of one particular family in the community. Their presence was quite noticeable: they littered the parking lots, carved graffiti in the picnic tables, and broke the speed limit. Ominous strangers showed up at dusk to party in the park, even though a curfew had been set. Things were so bad that board members resigned and residents began selling their homes.

The association considered their options: they could fine the parents (who didn't speak English)—or perhaps irritate them with a stream of warning letters; file a lawsuit, which would probably touch off a long, costly, vitriolic battle; press criminal charges; or just live with the situation.

None of these solutions seemed right. Warning letters can create barriers to communication and exacerbate an existing problem. Lawsuits disrupt life, affect home sales, and they can be costly. Restraining orders couldn't be gotten on non-resident strangers, and doing nothing was ruled out.

One option remained on the table: alternative dispute resolution (ADR). I reviewed ADR methods with them, but they were afraid to meet face-to-face. I filed an injunction, the judge recommended ADR, and then scheduled the hearing a month later to "give the parties an opportunity to resolve this through ADR." If the parties didn't attempt to work things out through ADR, the judge said it would affect his decision at the hearing. I wasn't surprised; the courts in California have been pushing hard for ADR in recent years.

## Mediation

There are many types of alternative dispute resolution, but in this case, mediation seemed to be the best route.

All five board members, the parents, and three teenage sons gathered for the session, which was tense but eventually positive. The setting was safe and neutral, the mediator kept control of the process, and all participants had a chance to explain their positions, fears, and desires.

After board members expressed their concerns, the youngest son spoke up, surprising everyone. He said he was guilt-stricken by the difficulties that he and his older brothers were causing their parents, who did not speak English. Their parents were not wealthy, he explained, yet they had to incur these expenses and take time off work to attend the mediation. The teenager addressed the board directly and he apologized.

Everyone agreed to very limited uses of the park by the brothers and their friends, and each side agreed to pay their own attorney's fees. The agreement was submitted as a stipulated judgment. Shortly thereafter, the teenagers changed their behavior and complied with the agreement.

The impetus for this settlement was simple: No one wanted things to proceed any further through the legal system. Legal costs for a protracted court battle could have cost over $50,000. In this case, costs were about $4,000. The mediator's services cost approximately $2,000, and each side paid half. The balance covered attorney's fees. ADR also saved time—the entire process took just a few months. Legal battles can drag on for years.

## Use of ADR on the Rise

It's clear that people are looking for alternatives to costly, painful court battles. Employers are including ADR clauses in employment agreements. When disputes pit neighbor against neighbor, ADR preserves relationships in the community where people have to live together, in close proximity, for a long time.

Most states promote ADR within the courts or through special arbitration or mediation programs. In California, for example, a portion of all court-filing fees goes to local dispute-resolution groups to ensure that communities have low-cost ADR services available. The CAI Greater Houston chapter and the Better Business Bureau have a program that provides trained mediators to work on association disputes.

ADR doesn't work in every instance; still, it's less confrontational, less demanding, and more satisfying than litigation.

## Types of ADR

There are numerous ADR options available. Sometimes they're used in combination, integrated with litigation, or used during litigation. Association attorneys and managers can advise associations whether ADR is appropriate and which type is best.

### Mediation

Perhaps the best-kept secret and least-understood ADR process is mediation, which makes use of a neutral third party as a facilitator. A mediator guides disputants through an informal process that identifies everyone's interests and encourages people to communicate with each other in a safe, confidential setting.

In mediation, participants sign confidentiality statements agreeing not to repeat what was said in the session or use it in court against the other party. The goal of mediation is to help people find their own solution; but, it's a non-binding process, meaning that the participants have other options if it doesn't work.

Mediation is useful when one person has an ongoing

relationship with the other—for example, as neighbors, family members, or employers and employees. It is among the least expensive alternatives for resolving a disagreement, and one of the most successful, especially when people want to resolve the dispute. The success rate for mediation ranges from 65 percent for court-referred mediations to 90 percent for private mediations. Speed is another advantage; association disputes can be settled in three to four hours.

### Binding Arbitration

Binding arbitration is just that: binding. An arbitration session is held, the arbitrator renders a decision, which is presented for court approval, and a court order makes the decision enforceable. Occasionally, binding-arbitration is subject to judicial review.

Some people fear that arbitrators have more power than judges and none of the accountability. Or they feel severely limited when the courts impose a decision. However, binding arbitration often saves the public more money and grief than can be easily quantified.

In most cases, the finality of binding arbitration is what makes the process so appealing. Trials and appeals can drag on seemingly forever, and costs become so prohibitive that it's easier to give up.

### Non-binding Arbitration

Decisions rendered in non-binding arbitration aren't binding until both parties agree with the decision; if they disagree, they don't have to accept it. Once they agree with the decision, however, that's the end of the process.

You can find yourself in non-binding arbitration because you chose it, or because you were thrust into the process by a contractual clause or judicial mandate. Depending on the level of damages, many court cases are directed to arbitration.

Arbitration proceedings are much like trials, but less formal. The arbitrator can consider testimony, hearsay, and records that would be excluded in a trial. In choosing non-binding arbitration, parties are generally indicating a desire for an inexpensive, quick resolution—often just an indication of dollars due. Thus, the decision is usually advisory in nature—but it's a good indication of what you could expect at trial.

**ARBITRATION.** Residents in an association complained about the swim team using the community's swimming pool. The board believed the CC&Rs allowed it, but when the association's attorney disagreed, the board instigated an arbitration proceeding to make a final determination. The arbitrator found that the CC&Rs didn't authorize the use and that an amendment would have to be approved by the members. It was done, and the measure was approved.

**MEDIATION.** One family's portable basketball hoop occasionally ended up in the street, which led to children playing in traffic. Sometimes it tipped over in the street. Worried about safety, the board decided that the portable unit violated association rules and had it removed. The family immediately reported the unit stolen and demanded that police arrest the board members. After mediation, everyone agreed on standards for using, maintaining, and storing the hoop.

**NEUTRAL EVALUATION.** When an owner withheld assessments because a leaky roof hadn't been repaired, the association filed a lien. The owner located a legal expert online, and the board agreed to neutral evaluation with the expert. The evaluator found that the law did not allow assessments to be withheld in such cases. The owner paid the assessments immediately.

**MEDIATION HYBRID.** A resident with a serious allergy was bothered by the pet dander left behind in the common elevator. The pet owner had a disability that required the use of a companion dog. A management consultant served as facilitator in a mediation type process and an agreement was reached. All three parties split the cost of extra vacuuming in the elevators and the hallways, and they worked out a schedule for using the elevator.

Many consider non-binding arbitration an unnecessary expense and a waste of time because there is no guaranteed resolution. This is a fair objection, but, in *binding* arbitration, the proceedings tend to be more adversarial; each side is much more invested because of the permanence of the decision.

**Hybrids of Mediation and Arbitration**

Sometimes it's appropriate to use both arbitration and mediation for the same case. For example, a neutral third party first tries to mediate the dispute, then, if that is unsuccessful, makes a decision that may or may not involve arbitration. Or the process can be reversed: The third party arbitrates the dispute, and then seals

the decision until the parties go through mediation. If the dispute isn't resolved through mediation, the decision—which the parties have agreed to accept—is unsealed.

Courts or contracts don't usually impose hybrid arrangements; rather, the involved parties agree to them. Courts normally won't recommend hybrids because they raise difficulties for the mediator regarding confidentiality and potential conflicts. For example, if a person admits guilt to the facilitator during a confidential meeting allowed in mediation, and then the process shifts from mediation to arbitration, the confidential admission of guilt could be used to render an adverse decision.

### Negotiation

In a negotiation, the disputing parties themselves—and in some cases their attorneys—work out a solution in writing, by phone, or in face-to-face meetings. The parties have complete control over the proceedings, which can lead to a written, enforceable agreement, an oral agreement, or something as simple as a new understanding. Negotiations can be friendly or heated; it's best to try this alternative first, and work with the other party until negotiations break down. For reasonable people who are able (and willing) to listen, understand, empathize, and communicate, negotiation is often successful. The least formal and most private of the ADR processes, negotiation is also usually the least expensive, and generally promotes the most cooperative resolution.

### Conciliation

A conciliator is a neutral third party who helps facilitate communication during a dispute. Conciliation can produce the same sorts of agreements that are made through negotiation or mediation, with the facilitator (conciliator) helping the parties arrive at their own resolution. A difference between conciliation and mediation, however, is that a conciliator can be anyone mutually chosen or accepted by the parties. Formalities of confidentiality agreements and a specific mediation process are usually absent in conciliation. A conciliator is often someone who simply can help the parties remain peaceful so they can discuss matters (e.g., a counselor), or someone who might make suggestions (e.g., a minister). Sometimes conciliation amounts to an agreement to settle based on the opinion of a specially chosen, expert, neutral person.

### Neutral Evaluation

This process can be used if the parties agree to it. A neutral evaluator—often an attorney—may meet with the parties to evaluate the case, including its monetary value, assess the strengths and weaknesses of each person's arguments, and review the goals. The evaluator tries to help the participants arrive at a settlement. The evaluator, chosen for his or her level of expertise, represents neither party individually and is trusted because of that neutrality.

People agree to this process when they desire a fair resolution and when everyone trusts the evaluator's decision. The process is neither binding nor enforceable. Since lack of knowledge is often at the root of community association disputes, this process helps when people don't want to talk or make difficult decisions without knowledgeable advice.

### Settlement Conference

When disputants are close to trial, a court may order them to participate in a settlement conference conducted by a court-appointed judge or attorney. Some judges and attorneys take a heavy-handed approach—"You're not leaving this room until you reach a settlement, even if it takes all night." Others are more flexible and will caucus with each party and attorney separately.

### Fact Finding

Neutral third parties also help by gathering information about the issues in question. For example, California has a procedure in which the facts can be submitted to the court, eliminating the need for discovery, a protracted trial, or a drawn-out legal battle. The judge merely applies law to the facts and renders a judgment. This is a great example of how ADR can be coupled with a legal proceeding to save time and money.

## Which One Is Right for You?

ADR is not a one-size-fits-all solution. As you can see, there are many ways to approach solving community association problems using these methods. Each circumstance is different and your attorney and/or manager can help guide you. In my opinion, if you really want to settle a dispute, you would do well to submit to mediation. If you just want to win, no matter what the cost, or if you want to rely on your attorney, or have someone else tell you what to do, arbitration or even litigation might be for you. (After all, that's often what the latter two forums are about—relinquishing the opportunity to make your own decisions.)

Few disputes are so all-or-nothing that there isn't room for settling differences through intercessions or friendly intervention. Even the most emotionally charged situations can be resolved through means other than litigation, if the parties are given the opportunity. Our courts will always be an important and invaluable resource, but it's critical that you choose your court battles wisely…and don't overlook *any* of your options.

## MY PERSPECTIVE

**Beth A. Grimm** is an attorney with Beth A. Grimm Professional Law Corporation.

*Over several years of experience representing associations, and serving as a volunteer mediator, I've seen all types of ADR in action. Again, each circumstance is different, but I would have to say that mediation is consistently the winner.*

*After mediation, the parties may not be in complete agreement, but they usually will be able to talk to each other again. The process is very empowering because people have an opportunity to be part of the solution instead of being ordered to comply with an outsiders' best stab at a solution. People have ownership in the outcome.*

*Arbitration has its role, but it worries me. In California, for example, the decision of an arbitrator is not challengeable in the courts. Even if they don't follow the law or if they make mistakes, the decision cannot be overturned. Many attorneys prefer arbitration because it results in a clear-cut decision. However, I believe this method carries the most risk.*